THE ESSENTIAL COLLE

CLASSIC FILM

GOLD

Published by:
Chester Music Limited,
8/9 Frith Street, London W1D 3JB, England.

Exclusive Distributors:
Music Sales Limited,
Distribution Centre, Newmarket Road, Bury St Edmunds, Suffolk IP33 3YB, England.
Music Sales Corporation,
257 Park Avenue South, New York, NY10010, United States of America.
Music Sales Pty Limited,
120 Rothschild Avenue, Rosebery, NSW 2018, Australia.

Order No. CH69256
ISBN 1-84449-780-1
This book © Copyright 2005 by Chester Music.

Arranging and engraving supplied by Camden Music.

Printed in the United Kingdom.

Your Guarantee of Quality:
As publishers, we strive to produce every book to the highest commercial standards.
The music has been freshly engraved and carefully designed to minimise
awkward page turns to make playing from it a real pleasure.
Particular care has been given to specifying acid-free, neutral-sized
paper made from pulps which have not been elemental chlorine bleached.
This pulp is from farmed sustainable forests and was produced
with special regard for the environment.
Throughout, the printing and binding have been planned to ensure a sturdy,
attractive publication which should give years of enjoyment.
If your copy fails to meet our high standards, please inform us and we will gladly replace it.

www.musicsales.com

CHESTER MUSIC
part of the Music Sales Group

London/New York/Paris/Sydney/Copenhagen/Berlin/Madrid/Tokyo

The Essential Collection: Classic Film Gold

'Film music' originated as a preferred counterpoint to the silent film's clacking projector and as a means of contributing emotion and action through an aural medium. Some films provided a catalogue of musical excerpts to suit specific emotions, performed by whatever resources were to hand. Otherwise, the Victorian era's popularity of the piano ensured that enough scraps of established classical repertoire could still be found in any piano bench, to suit any number of emotions and circumstances. In retrospect, these musical snippets were nothing short of formulaic clichés, performed on an out-of-tune upright, the town hall's organ, or if you were really lucky, by a full orchestra. Thankfully, the silver screen's world of sound evolved, and with the film, 'King Kong' of 1933, came the realisation that an original score could radically enhance any film. From the rubble of New York City after the giant ape's arms had stopped thrashing, emerged a landmark symphonic score by Max Steiner. For any film, attention to the music became as integral as the lighting or the cinematography, and opening credits soon included the names of Steiner, Franz Waxman and Erich Wolfgang Korngold, emigrated Europeans who had received classical training in the German tradition.

The next 30 years regularly drew on the classics for theme music: for example, 'Flash Gordon' blared out Franz Liszt's *Les Preludes* to spluttering spacecraft and Tchaikovsky's *Romeo and Juliet* to swooping romantic interludes, while Orson Welles signed on and off the radio with the opening of Tchaikovsky's *First Piano Concerto*. By the 1950s, American-born composers such as Alfred Newman (uncle of Randy, father of Thomas and David), David Raksin, Victor Young, Bernard Herrmann, Dimitri Tiomkin, Miklos Rozsa and Elmer Bernstein, could all manipulate an audience with commendable skill via traditional composing techniques. In no other art-form could a set of aesthetic formulas be so eagerly copied and adapted—Tiomkin is famous for his Oscar acceptance speech for scoring the 1954 film, 'The High and the Mighty': "I would like to thank Johannes Brahms, Johann Strauss, Richard Strauss, Richard Wagner, Beethoven…"

In 1968, 'The Graduate' offered a score that was part pre-existing Simon and Garfunkel, and part original Dave Grusin. As the costs of film production started to get a bit feisty, Hollywood producers fast-realised the financial benefits of utilising music that was already in existence, rather than commissioning a composer with his 100-piece orchestra. Films in the 1970s suddenly became cluttered with wall-to-wall Top-40 hits—until John Williams let rip with his fantastic, original and symphonic score for 'Star Wars'.

To a certain extent little has changed in film music since its evolution: budgets determine a great deal; credit music often features a big solo name as a marketing ploy (Celine Dion in 'Titanic' was a good move); formulaic music is employed to accompany the good, the bad, the love, the comical, the character, the location and the scene change. *All* the music is there to manipulate the observer in some cunning and subliminal way. However, the actual method of 'discovering the *right* music' for any one moment of a film during its production stage can be an interesting and unique story!

Most directors edit their films to a 'temp track'—a 'musical stand-in' if you like—that is often a compilation drawn from someone's collection of CD classical warhorses, or even from the latest successful movie. It enables the production team to get a feel for the film's direction as they edit away, to help make sense of the film at its preview-screening stage, and to give the composer some indicators as to the nature of the desired music. A skilled film composer will then create original music that can hit and emphasise any number of dramatic points in a scene, ultimately creating a stronger finished product due to its fusion and focus. But we know how attractive familiarity can be, and with directors, upon occasion, falling in love with their temp tracks, the commissioned composer's work has often been ditched. The use of pre-existent music also makes the film's production process significantly faster, easier and cheaper.

Who knows if the classical titles in this book were actually intended by the directors to be temp tracks in their films or whether the directors started filming with this music already in mind? All of these classics have been around for over 100 years, and yet have been a significant feature of contemporary film.

What is remarkable, is that the classic piece of music, with its wholly predetermined mood, can be given a renaissance by being wedded to a radically new visual partner—for example, in 'Apocalypse Now' Colonel Kilgore mounts speakers to the helicopters, and it is Wagner that gets to score the resulting horrific insanity; the 'Air Cavalry' napalms an entire South East Asian village to the tune of *Ride of the Valkyries*, once a bit of opera. 'The Big Lebowski' uses Mozart's *Requiem* in the scene where Jeffrey Lebowski sobbingly tells 'The Dude' of his wife's kidnapping; 'The Dude' couldn't care less and absent-mindedly asks him, "Mind if I do a 'J'?" At the end of 'Ocean's 11', music shifts the gear as the gang looks out over the city before going their separate ways. What better way to conclude the perfectly executed heist than with the flowing piano music of Debussy's *Clair De Lune*, his best-loved piano piece, which has been used in many a film, and is still sounding fresh while that clacking projector fades into history.

Quentin Thomas, March 2005

• Vidor's Toccata.
• Wachet Auf.

APOCALYPSE NOW
The Ride of the Valkyries
(from Die Walküre)

Composed by Richard Wagner
Arranged by Jerry Lanning

Vivace ♩. = 96

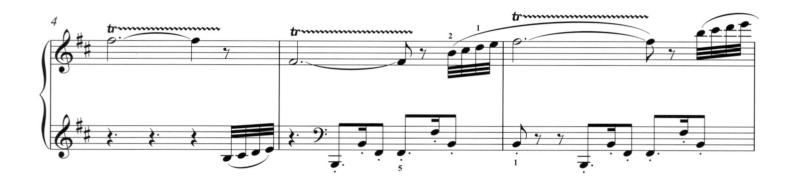

ARTIFICIAL INTELLIGENCE: A.I.
Waltz
(from The Sleeping Beauty)

Composed by Pyotr Ilyich Tchaikovsky

Arranged by Jerry Lanning

Allegro (Tempo di valse) ♩. = 68

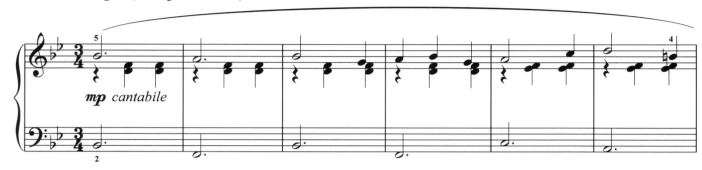

11

THE AVIATOR
Toccata and Fugue in D minor

Composed by Johann Sebastian Bach

Arranged by Jerry Lanning

BIG FISH
Symphony No.6 'Pastoral'
(Allegretto theme)

Composed by Ludwig van Beethoven
Arranged by Jack Long

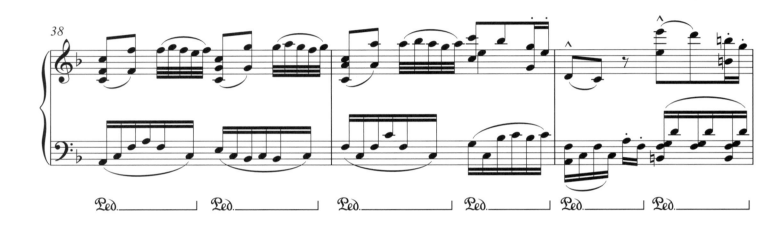

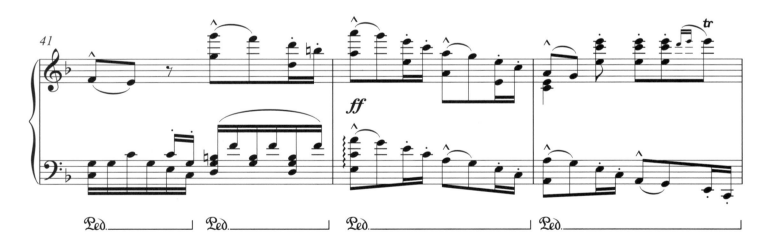

THE BIG LEBOWSKI
Lacrimosa
(from Requiem in D minor)
Composed by Wolfgang Amadeus Mozart

23

BRIDGET JONES'S DIARY
Hallelujah Chorus
(from Messiah)

Composed by George Frideric Handel

ELIZABETH
Requiem Aeternam
(from Requiem in D minor)

Composed by Wolfgang Amadeus Mozart
Arranged by Quentin Thomas

CAPTAIN CORELLI'S MANDOLIN
La Donna È Mobile
(from Rigoletto)

Composed by Giuseppe Verdi
Arranged by Jerry Lanning

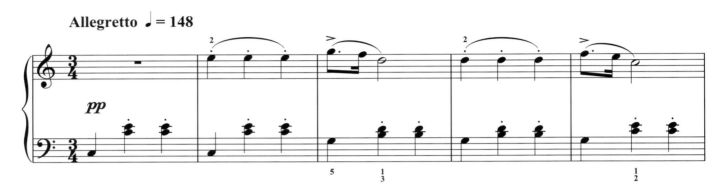

CLOSER
Soave Sia Il Vento
(from Cosi Fan Tutte)

Composed by Wolfgang Amadeus Mozart

Arranged by Quentin Thomas

THE FINAL CUT
Spring (1st movement)
(from The Four Seasons)

Composed by Antonio Vivaldi
Arranged by Barry Todd

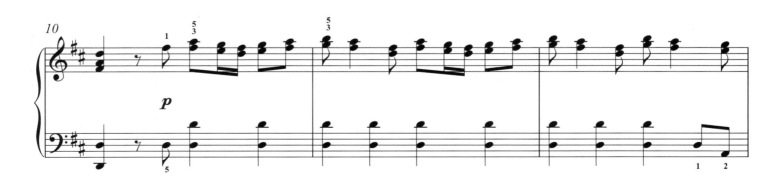

FOUR WEDDINGS AND A FUNERAL
The Arrival of the Queen of Sheba
(from Solomon)

Composed by George Frideric Handel

GODFATHER III
String Quartet No.2
(Theme from 3rd movement)

Composed by Alexander Borodin

L.A. CONFIDENTIAL
Hebrides Overture 'Fingal's Cave'

Composed by Felix Mendelssohn
Arranged by Quentin Thomas

MINORITY REPORT
Jesu, Joy of Man's Desiring
(from Cantata 147)

Composed by Johann Sebastian Bach
Arranged by Jerry Lanning

Moderato ♩ = 80

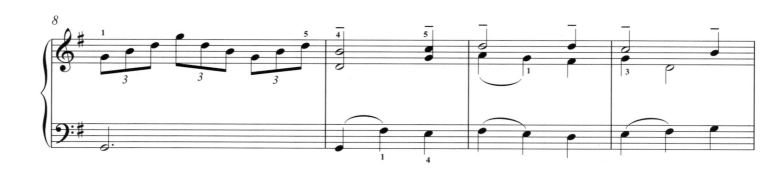

rall. poco a poco

OCEAN'S ELEVEN
Clair De Lune
(from Suite Bergamasque)

Composed by Claude Debussy

Tempo I

58

pp *morendo jusqu'à la fin*

OCEAN'S TWELVE
Symphony No.3 'Eroica'
(4th movement opening: Allegro molto)

Composed by Ludwig van Beethoven

Arranged by Quentin Thomas

LEMONY SNICKET'S 'A SERIES OF UNFORTUNATE EVENTS'
Hungarian Dance No.5

Composed by Johannes Brahms
Arranged by Quentin Thomas

THE OTHERS
Waltz in A♭ major (Posthumous) Op.69, No.1

Composed by Frédéric Chopin

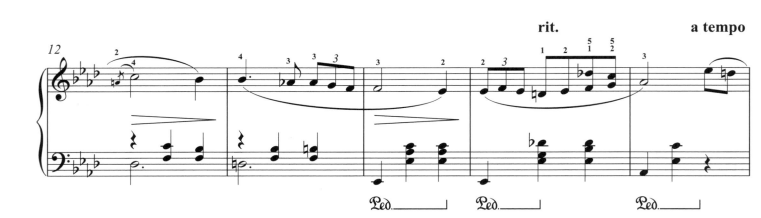

RAY
'Moonlight' Sonata Op.27, No.2

Composed by Ludwig van Beethoven

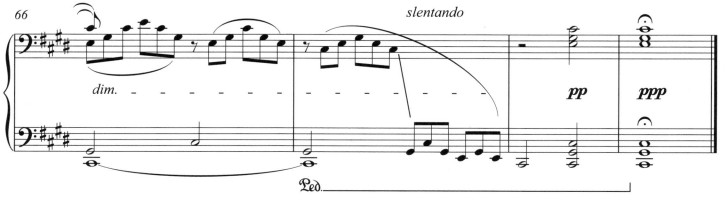

SHINE
Prélude in D♭ major 'Raindrop' Op.28, No.15

Composed by Frédéric Chopin
Arranged by Jack Long

smorz.

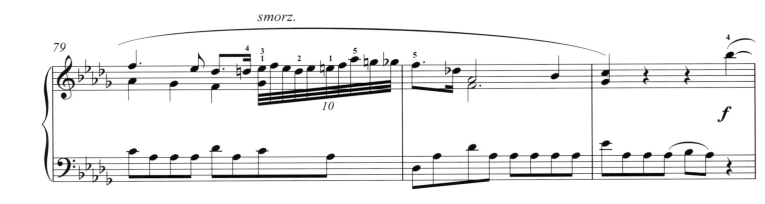

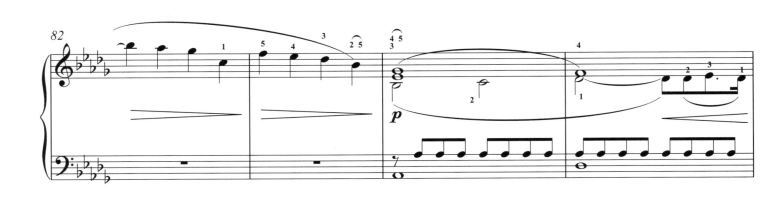

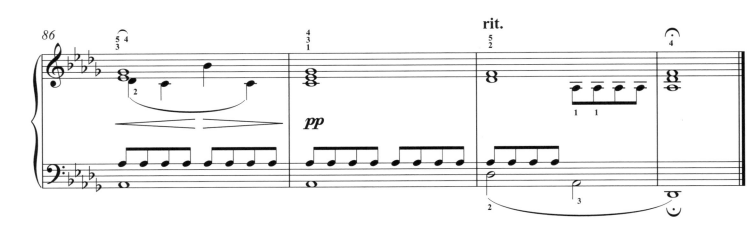

THE STING
The Entertainer

Composed by Scott Joplin

(repeat R.H. 8va. higher)

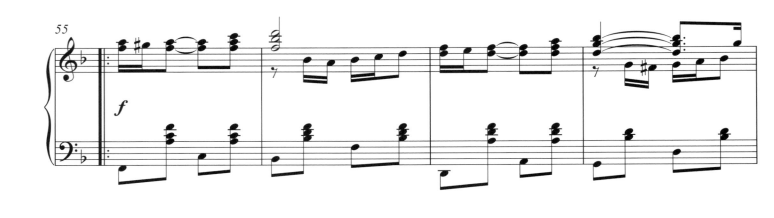

SIXTH SENSE
Trout Quintet Op.114
(4th movement: Andantino)

Composed by Franz Peter Schubert

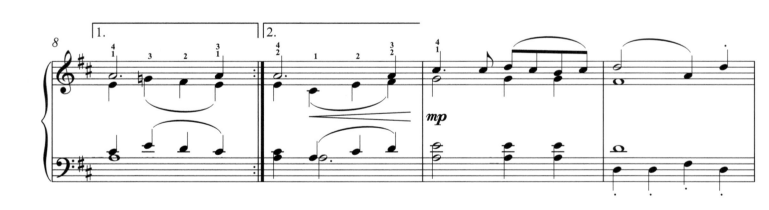

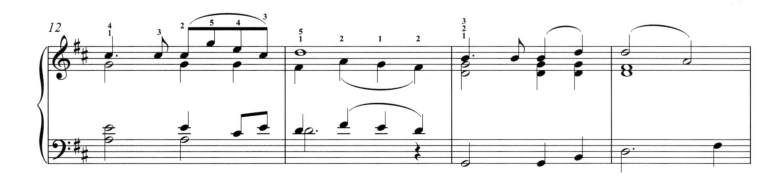

TEA WITH MUSSOLINI
Träumerei
(from Kinderszenen)

Composed by Robert Schumann

91

TITANIC
Meditation
(from Thaïs)

Composed by Jules Massenet
Arranged by Jerry Lanning

THE TALENTED MR. RIPLEY
'Stabat Mater dolorosa'
(from Stabat Mater)

Composed by Antonio Vivaldi
Arranged by Quentin Thomas

123456789